CALIFORNIA

Janice Parker

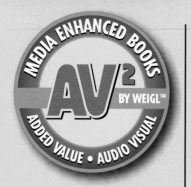

AV² provides enriched content that supplements and complements this book. Weigl's AV² books strive to create inspired learning and engage young minds in a total learning experience.

Your AV² Media Enhanced books come alive with...

Audio
Listen to sections of the book read aloud.

Key Words
Study vocabulary, and complete a matching word activity.

Video
Watch informative video clips.

Quizzes
Test your knowledge.

Embedded Weblinks
Gain additional information for research.

Slide Show
View images and captions, and prepare a presentation.

Try This!
Complete activities and hands-on experiments.

... and much, much more!

Go to **www.av2books.com**, and enter this book's unique code.

BOOK CODE

X226564

AV² by Weigl brings you media enhanced books that support active learning.

Published by AV² by Weigl
350 5th Avenue, 59th Floor
New York, NY 10118
Website: www.av2books.com

Library of Congress Cataloging-in-Publication Data
Names: Parker, Janice, author.
Title: California : the Golden State / Janice Parker.
Description: New York, NY : AV2 by Weigl, [2016] | Series: Discover America | Includes index.
Identifiers: LCCN 2015044634 (print) | LCCN 2015045174 (ebook) | ISBN 9781489648273 (hard cover : alk. paper) | ISBN 9781489648280 (soft cover : alk. paper) | ISBN 9781489648297 (Multi-User eBook)
Subjects: LCSH: California--Juvenile literature.
Classification: LCC F861.3 .P375 207 (print) | LCC F861.3 (ebook) | DDC 979.4--dc23
LC record available at http://lccn.loc.gov/2015044634

Printed in the United States of America, in Brainerd, Minnesota
1 2 3 4 5 6 7 8 9 20 19 18 17 16

042016
040816

Project Coordinator Heather Kissock
Art Director Terry Paulhus

Photo Credits
Every reasonable effort has been made to trace ownership and to obtain permission to reprint copyright material. The publisher would be pleased to have any errors or omissions brought to their attention so that they may be corrected in subsequent printings. The publisher acknowledges Getty Images, Corbis Images, Dreamstime, and Alamy as its primary image suppliers for this title.

CALIFORNIA

Contents

STATE TREE
California Redwood

STATE FLOWER
California Poppy

STATE FLAG
California

STATE GEMSTONE
Benitoite

STATE BIRD
California Quail

STATE SEAL
California

Nickname
The Golden State

Motto
Eureka
(I Have Found It)

Song
"I Love You, California,"
words by F.B. Silverwood and
music by Alfred Frankenstein

Population
(2014 Census) 38,802,500
Ranked 1st state

Capital
Sacramento

Entered the Union
September 9, 1850, as the 31st state

Discover California

California's warm climate, beautiful landscapes, exciting attractions, and economic opportunities draw people from around the world. California has the most residents of any U.S. state, with more than 38 million people. Beautiful beaches, rocky cliffs, snowy mountains, barren deserts, and lush forests are all within close distance from one another.

California is well known for its entertainment industry. Many of the world's motion pictures and television programs are created and filmed in the state. The center of the movie and TV industry is Hollywood, a district in Los Angeles. Movie stars are a common sight in some California cities. People from all over the world move to California with dreams of becoming successful in show business.

California is known for its national parks, such as Joshua Tree, Sequoia National Park, and Death Valley. The state's large and varied economy is a major reason people choose to relocate to California. Many people looking for a healthy and active lifestyle enjoy the mild weather, and fresh fruits and vegetables.

The Land

Big Sur is an area located on the Pacific Ocean. Most of the area is either privately owned or part of the state park system.

California is the most biologically diverse state, with more than **40,000** plant and animal species.

California's nickname, **the Golden State**, is thanks to the 1849 **gold rush** and the fields of **golden poppies** found in the state.

Beginnings

There are several theories about the origin of the state's name, but many people believe it came from a Spanish novel written in the 1500s. The book described a fictional island east of Asia called California. This island was rumored to have mountains of gold and other precious gems.

When the Europeans first arrived, there were an estimated 130,000 Native Americans already living in California. The land was claimed by Spain, but for two centuries there were only a few explorers and **missionaries** who settled in California. This changed in the latter half of the eighteenth century, when land routes were opened between California and other major Spanish territories in Arizona and New Mexico.

After gold was discovered in California, more than 80,000 prospectors made their way to the state in just one year.

California became a Mexican territory after Mexico's War of Independence in 1821. By this time, many Mexicans and Americans were living in the territory. Tensions rose, sparking the conflict known as the Mexican-American War in 1846. The war ended in 1848 with the Treaty of Guadalupe Hidalgo, which gave California, as well as present day Arizona, Utah, Colorado, Nevada, New Mexico, and Wyoming to the United States.

One year later, in 1849, California saw one of the largest gold rushes in world history. The gold rush began when James Marshall found gold near Sutter's Mill, a sawmill in Coloma owned by John Sutter. After that, people from all over the world flocked to California. This large influx of people helped set California on the fast track to statehood, which came only one year later in 1850.

Where is CALIFORNIA?

C alifornia is bordered by Nevada and Arizona to the east, Oregon to the north, and Mexico to the south. The western border is defined by the Pacific Ocean. California has the second-longest coastline in the **contiguous** United States, after Florida. Its coastline is 840 miles long.

United States Map

California

Alaska   Hawaiʻi

MAP LEGEND

- California
- ☆ Capital City
- ● Major City
- Death Valley
- Yosemite
- Bordering States
- Mexico
- Water

N

SCALE   0   100 miles

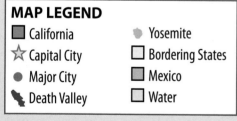

1 Sacramento

Sacramento, with a population of more than 479,000, became California's state capital in 1854. Previous capitals were San Jose, Vallejo, and Benicia. Sacramento is in north-central California, about 88 miles northeast of San Francisco Bay.

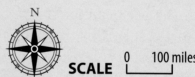

2 Death Valley

Death Valley, which includes Death Valley National Park, is the hottest and driest place in North America. Despite its extreme conditions, a wide diversity of ecosystems exist. Salt fields, dry parched land, sand dunes, mountains, and a lake that lies below sea level create a unique landscape in this remote valley.

OREGON

IDAHO

WYOMING

UTAH

NEVADA

⭐ **Sacramento**

1

3

2

CALIFORNIA

ARIZONA

4

Pacific Ocean

San Diego

MEXICO

3 Yosemite

Perhaps one of the most beautiful places in California, Yosemite National Park encompasses 1,189 square miles of pristine wilderness. It is home to the impressive rock formation Half Dome, as well as many iconic animals of the West, including black bears, coyotes, bighorn sheep, and pumas.

4 San Diego

The second-largest city in California after Los Angeles, San Diego has a large tourist industry. Along with its pristine coastline and 70-degree weather, the city features attractions such as Seaworld and the San Diego Zoo. It also features many unique neighborhoods, including the Gaslamp Quarter and Little Italy.

Land Features

California is a land of contrasts. It contains both the highest and lowest points in the 48 contiguous U.S. states, and includes fertile valleys, forests, sandy beaches, arid deserts, and extensive mountain ranges. Much of the eastern part of the state is a desert region. Mountain ranges, such as the Sierra Nevada, run down the center of the state. Other major mountain ranges in the state are the Klamath Mountains, in northwestern California, and the southern part of the Cascade Range.

Mojave Desert

California's largest desert, the Mojave, covers more than 25,000 square miles. It also spreads into Nevada, Arizona, and Utah. Death Valley, a popular location in the Mojave, is the lowest point both in California and the continental United States.

San Andreas Fault

The San Andreas Fault is a fracture in Earth's surface that runs north to south through the state for more than 800 miles. Earthquakes often occur along this fault.

Mount Whitney

The highest point in California is Mount Whitney. At 14,494 feet, it is also the highest point in the continental U.S.

Central Valley

The great Central Valley, which runs 450 miles from north to south and covers about 18,000 square miles, is almost completely enclosed by mountains.

Climate

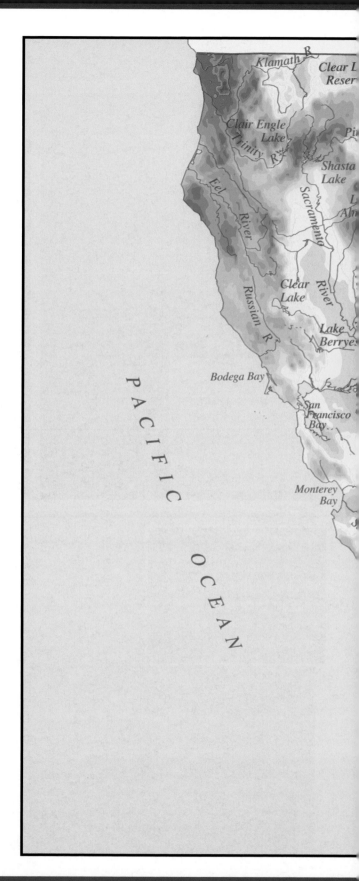

With so many landscapes, California also has many different climates. Southern coastal areas are sunny with mild winters. Northern coastal areas are also mild but cooler. The valley and foothill areas are hot and dry in the summer, and cold and humid in the winter. The desert areas are very dry and hot.

The average temperature in California is about 44° Fahrenheit in January and about 75°F in July. Temperatures vary considerably, however. In Susanville, in mountainous northeastern California, the average temperature in January is 31°F, and in July it is 69°F.

Average Annual Precipitation Across California

California's annual precipitation averages about 22 inches per year, but the amount varies greatly by region. In general, rain falls mainly in the winter. Why might some areas of the state receive much more rainfall than others?

LEGEND

Average Annual Precipitation (in inches) 1961–1990

 200 – 100.1

100 – 25.1

25 – 5 and less

Goose
Lake

Upper Lake

Middle Alkali
Lake

River

Eagle
Lake

or

Honey
Lake

ake
Oroville

Lake
Tahoe

NEVADA

UTAH

Mokelumne R.

Stanislaus R.

San Joaquin

Merced

River

Kings

Front-Kern Canal

Mono
Lake

Owens

River

Owens
Lake

River

Kern

nas R.

Buena Vista
Lake

Amargosa R.

Lake
Havasu

ARIZONA

Santa Barbara
Channel

San Pedro Channel

Outer Santa Barbara
Passage

Salton
Sea

Coachella Canal

Colorado R.

Nature's Resources

Timber is an important natural resource in California. Almost 40 percent of the state is covered with forests. Among the most common trees are firs, pines, and oaks.

The state is rich in marine life such as crabs and tuna. Fish and shellfish, including lobsters and shrimp, are caught off the coast of California. Other economically important catches include sardines, salmon, rockfish, black cod, sole, swordfish, and urchin.

The timber harvest brings in nearly $900 million to California's economy.

California's minerals are another important resource. Cement, sand, gravel, and stone are mined in **quarries** and used throughout the United States. California's beaches and other recreation areas are an important resource for tourism. The state's abundant rivers and lakes provide irrigation for agriculture and power through **hydroelectricity**.

Petroleum production has been an important industry since the beginning of the twentieth century. California led the nation in petroleum production between 1900 and 1936. Even though production has slowed, it remains a profitable resource, generating more income than all of the mineral industries combined.

The California spiny lobster lives off the coast in the Pacific Ocean, from Monterey to the Gulf of Tehuantepec in Mexico.

The Shasta Dam crosses the Sacramento River. The dam created Lake Shasta, which is the third largest body of water in California.

Vegetation

California's plant life is as varied as its geography and climate. Northern California has woodlands that contain some of the world's tallest trees, the coastal redwoods. Giant sequoia trees in the Sierra Nevada are the largest of all trees in bulk. Their trunks can sometimes measure up to 40 feet across. Other common trees are oak, aspen, palm, and eucalyptus. Common plants found in California are the flowering dogwood and myrtle.

The desert areas contain many different species of **succulents**. The state flower, the golden poppy, grows in the Central Valley. Creosote and mesquite are some of the few plants that can survive in the hot, dry climate of Death Valley.

California Redwood

Also known as the coast redwood, these massive trees can reach heights of more than 350 feet.

Bristlecone Pine Tree

These unusual-looking trees grow in the White Mountains. One bristlecone pine, nicknamed Methuselah, is thought to be more than 4,700 years old.

Joshua Tree

The Joshua tree is the largest member of the yucca family. These trees can be found in the southeastern part of the state.

California Poppy

The California poppy was designated California's state flower in 1903. Residents celebrate April 6th as California Poppy Day.

Wildlife

California is home to many different types of animals. Marine animals, such as otters, seals, and whales, can be found off the coast. Coyotes, hares, and lizards roam in desert areas. Cougars, black bears, and bobcats live in the forests. Many different bird species spend all or part of the year in California. Seagulls, terns, and pelicans live along the coast. Spotted owls live in the northern forests.

The California condor is one of the largest species of bird in the world and is iconic in California. It can fly at speeds of up to 55 miles per hour. Though there were once hundreds throughout the state, human habitation destroyed their **habitat**, and the condors began to die out. In 1982, there were only about 20 of the birds left, and they are considered **endangered**. **Conservation** groups have tried to save the California condor by breeding birds in **captivity**. Today, there are about 160 California condors living in nature. Several other California animals are endangered, including the riparian brush rabbit, the San Joaquin kit fox, and several species of kangaroo rats.

Sea Lion

California is home to nearly 240,000 sea lions. Groups of these playful animals can be seen in many coastal areas.

Desert Cottontail

The desert cottontail is the most common rabbit found in California's deserts and valleys. Cottontails avoid extreme heat by resting in the shade on hot summer days.

Bighorn Sheep

The Sierra Nevada bighorn sheep was listed as an endangered species in California in 2000. The sheep usually live on rocky or grassy mountain slopes and are skillfull climbers.

California Quail

The state bird of California is known for the curved black crown feather on its forehead. This ground-dwelling bird adapts easily to different environments and lives throughout the state.

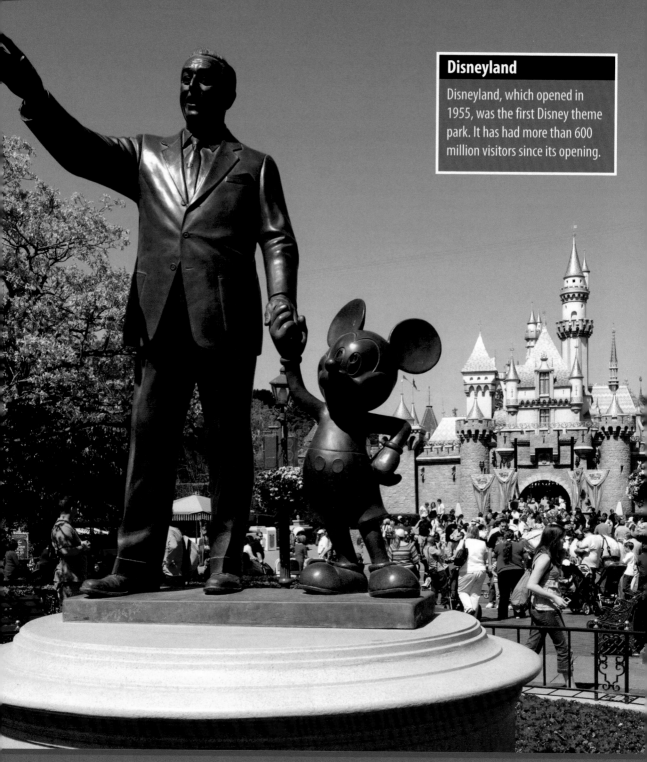

Economy

Tourism

Tourism is an important industry in California, contributing more than $87 billion annually to the state's economy. The state's eight national parks are some of the most popular in the country. Los Angeles, San Francisco, and San Diego attract many visitors from across the country and around the world. Families come to visit the state's many amusement parks and zoos.

Many people come to California for its coastline. They enjoy the beautiful beaches and sports such as surfing, windsurfing, and sailing. Visitors may drive along scenic Highway 1, which follows the shoreline for much of the way between San Francisco and Los Angeles. Along this drive is Big Sur, a 100-mile-long, ruggedly beautiful stretch of seacoast.

Golden Gate Bridge

The Golden Gate Bridge, completed in 1937, is one of San Francisco's most popular tourist attractions. It is estimated that 9 million people visit the bridge every year.

San Diego Zoo

Known for the care it takes to reproduce natural habitats, the San Diego Zoo is one of the most popular zoos in the world. It is home to more than 4,000 animals, including giant pandas.

Hollywood

Hollywood, in Los Angeles, is considered the center of the U.S. film industry. Visitors come to the area to take tours and see the homes of movie stars.

The headquarters of Apple Inc. is located in Cupertino, California. In 2015, the company made more than $233 billion.

Primary Industries

Manufacturing, tourism, and agriculture are some of the leading industries in California. The entertainment industry provides jobs for many Californians. Actors, directors, screenwriters, camera operators, and special-effects staff all help to create films and television shows.

Along the southern shores of San Francisco Bay is Silicon Valley, an area famous for its industry. The nickname is derived from the material silicon, which is used to make microchips for computers and other electronic equipment. Today, many major technology companies call Silicon Valley home. Google, Facebook, and Apple are all headquartered there.

More than half of the **fruits** and **vegetables** produced in the United States are grown in California.

The **well-known jeans** brand **Levi's** started in San Francisco in **1873,** and is still headquartered there today.

Value of Goods and Services (in Millions of Dollars)

California is known for its entertainment and technology industries, but workers in the state are employed in many different fields. Why might health care be such a large industry?

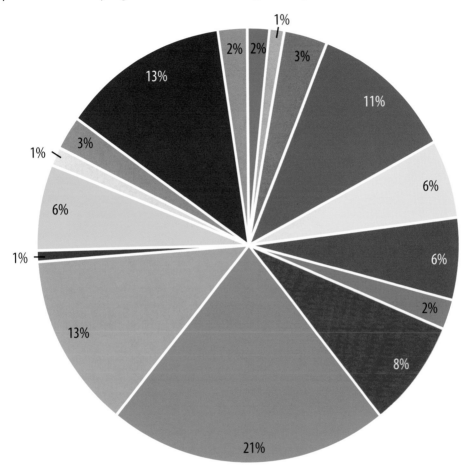

Agriculture, forestry, fishing	$37,345	
Mining	$26,143	
Construction	$71,074	
Manufacturing	$244,629	
Wholesale Trade	$129,600	
Retail Trade	$129,298	
Transportation and Warehousing	$50,537	
Information and Publishing	$176,168	
Finance, Insurance, Real Estate	$465,897	
Professional and Business Services	$285,957	
Education	$22,101	
Healthcare and Social Assistance	$138,248	
Arts and Entertainment	$28,697	
Hotels and Restaurants	$56,750	
Government	$275,233	
Other Services	$47,649	

Goods and Services

The service sector accounts for a large portion of the jobs in California. Someone who works in the service sector provides a service for someone else. Service jobs are varied, including actors, social workers, government employees, doctors, schoolteachers, and bus drivers.

Agriculture is vital to the state's economy. California's more than 80,000 farms produce large quantities of nuts, fruits, and vegetables. Leading agricultural products include milk and grapes. Almost all of the pomegranates, walnuts, raisin, and olives in the U.S. are grown in California. The state also produces more greenhouse and nursery products, such as potted plants and cut flowers, than any other state.

Nursery plants generate about $3 million each year to California's agricultural economy.

California is a leading U.S. state for manufacturing. Factories make aircraft, ships, military supplies, electrical equipment, and chemicals. California also has many food processing plants, and publishing and printing businesses.

California produces more gold than most other states, and gold mining has played an important role in the history of the state. Shortly after California became a U.S. territory, gold was discovered. In 1849, people in search of gold came to California from all over the world. The people were called "forty-niners." The gold rush ended almost as quickly as it had begun, and had mostly ended by 1854.

California's grape harvesting season begins in late August and can run through October.

Tesla Motors, which builds fully electric cars, has a mission of creating a world that is less dependent on gas.

History

The Hupa have long been known for their basket making. The traditions of the past continue to be passed on to younger generations.

Native Americans

Scientists believe that, about 15,000 to 20,000 years ago, people crossed from what is now Siberia, in northern Asia, to North America by means of a land bridge that connected the two continents. That land bridge is now covered by the Bering Strait. Human beings then spread throughout North and South America, coming to occupy California probably by about 12,000 years ago. The prehistoric settlers in California were isolated from others on the continent by the high mountains. By the 1500s, the area that is now California had the greatest concentration of Native Americans in North America.

The early Native American groups in California included the Hupa, who lived in the far northwest. The Ohlone lived in the San Francisco area, and the Pomo lived to the north. The Maidu made their home in north-central California, and the Yuma, or Quechan, lived in the southernmost region. Some of the other native groups were the Cahuilla, Chumash, Karuk, Mojave, Yokuts, Paiute, and Modoc. The native people of California spoke many different languages and **dialects**, and usually coexisted peacefully.

Yuma women used pottery for carrying and storing food. They often painted red and black patterns on these containers.

Exploring the Land

On September 28, 1542, João Rodrigues Cabrilho, a Portuguese sailor, landed at San Diego Bay. He was the first European to reach what is now California. Cabrilho, who claimed the land for Spain, went on to explore the Catalina Islands, and sailed farther north to view the area that is now Santa Monica and the Channel Islands. In 1579, the British explorer Sir Francis Drake traveled to the San Francisco area. Drake claimed the land for Great Britain.

Timeline of Settlement

First Settlements

1769 The first Spanish mission, San Diego de Alcalá, is built in California.

1781 The city of Los Angeles is founded by the Spanish.

1602 Sebastian Vizcaíno sails from Mexico to explore the coast of California.

1812 A group of Russian fur traders and fur trappers establishes Fort Ross as a base for hunting and trading.

1579 Sir Francis Drake, a British explorer, travels to San Francisco. He claims the land, which he calls New Albion, for Great Britain.

1542 Portuguese sailor João Rodrigues Cabrilho lands at San Diego Bay. He is the first European to reach what is now California. Cabrilho claims the land for Spain.

Early Exploration

In the 1580s and 1590s, Francisco Gali and Sebastian Rodriguez Cermeño sailed along the northern California coast, exploring Cape Mendocino and Monterey Bay. In 1602, Sebastian Vizcaíno sailed to the coast of California. As he sailed, he named places such as San Diego, Catalina Island, Santa Barbara, and Monterey. He reported his findings to the Spanish king, urging him to create a colony in the area. It was not until 1769 that another Spanish **expedition** traveled to California.

1848 The Treaty of Guadalupe Hidalgo ends the Mexican-American War. Most of the Southwest, including California, is transferred from Mexico to the United States.

Gold and Statehood

1849 Hundreds of thousands of people flock to California after gold is discovered the year before. The gold was discovered at Sutter's Mill in Coloma.

1846 The Mexican-American War begins between the United States and Mexico.

1821 After 11 years of war, Mexico wins independence from Spain. Present-day California becomes part of Mexico.

Under Different Flags

1850 California becomes the 31st state on September 9th.

The mission at San Diego de Alcala is the first mission in California and was founded by Father Junipero Serra.

The First Settlers

Some of the first European settlers in California were Spanish missionaries. One of the most famous was Father Junipero Serra. The first Spanish mission in California was San Diego de Alcala, which was built near San Diego in 1769. Over the next half century, 20 other missions were built from San Diego to Sonoma. The Spanish built military forts, called presidios, near many of the missions. The missionaries tried to convert the Native Americans to Christianity. Many Native Americans resisted the beliefs and culture of the missionaries.

In 1812, a group of Russian fur traders moved south from Alaska to the northwest coast of California. They established Fort Ross, about 60 miles northeast of San Francisco, as a base for hunting seals and otters. Russian traders stayed until 1841, when they sold the fort to the U.S. pioneer Captain John A. Sutter.

In 1845, Captain John C. Frémont, a U.S. explorer and soldier, led an expedition to California. At the time, war seemed likely between the United States and Mexico due to a dispute over the border of Texas, which had recently become part of the United States. The conflict, known as the Mexican-American War, broke out in April 1846.

Less than two months later, in June, U.S. settlers near Sonoma revolted against Mexico and established the California Republic. Frémont supported the settlers and was elected leader of the republic. The republic fell quickly, as U.S. forces claimed California for the United States. In the Treaty of Guadalupe Hidalgo, which ended the Mexican-American War in 1848, Mexico gave control of California and the American Southwest to the United States.

Captain John Fremont became one of the first senators elected from California.

During the Treaty of Guadalupe Hidalgo, Mexico lost nearly half of its total territory.

History Makers

Many notable Californians contributed to development of their state and country. Ronald Reagan served as the 33rd governor of California before being elected president in 1980. Steve Jobs, the co-founder of Apple Inc., was born in San Francisco. Aviator Howard Hughes, later played by Leonardo DiCaprio in *The Aviator*, spent most of his life in Los Angeles.

William Randolph Hearst (1863–1951)

William Randolph Hearst was born to millionaire parents in San Francisco. While he was attending Harvard University, Hearst's father purchased the *San Francisco Examiner*. Hearst took over the newspaper from his father, and then began to acquire publications in other large cities. He later expanded to book publishing and magazines. Today, the Hearst Corporation is one of the largest communications companies in the world.

George Patton (1885–1945)

Born in San Gabriel township, George Patton was a United States Army officer who received the Purple Heart after his service in World War I. He became a household name during World War II when he helped successfully lead troops in North Africa, Sicily, and France, including in the Battle of the Bulge.

John Steinbeck (1902–1968)

Born in Salinas, John Steinbeck set many of his novels in California. He received the prestigious Pulitzer Prize for his book *The Grapes of Wrath* and was awarded the Nobel Prize for Literature in 1962. Steinbeck wrote more than 25 books in his career, including *East of Eden* and *Of Mice and Men*.

George Takei (1937–)

Los Angeles native George Takei is best known for playing Hikaru Sulu on the TV show *Star Trek*. After spending part of his childhood in a Japanese internment camp during World War II, Takei has worked to better the relationship between the United States and Japan.

Sally Ride (1951–2012)

Los Angeles-born Sally Ride attended Westlake High School and went on to Stanford University in Palo Alto. In 1978, she beat out 1,000 other applicants for a place in the National Aeronautics and Space Administration (NASA) astronaut program. In 1983, Ride became the first woman from the U.S. to go into space, aboard the space shuttle *Challenger*.

Culture

San Francisco's Chinatown is the largest Chinatown outside of Asia.

Downtown Los Angeles is the central business district of the city, but is also home to more than 50,000 Los Angeles residents.

The People Today

The majority of California's residents live in urban areas. Much of the population is centered in southern California, particularly from Los Angeles to San Diego. With more than 3.8 million residents, Los Angeles is California's largest city, and the second-largest city in the United States, after New York City. San Diego, the second-largest city in California, is home to more than 1.3 million people. Other major cities include Fresno, Long Beach, Oakland, Sacramento, San Francisco, and San Jose.

California is one of the most ethnically diverse states in the country. The Hispanic population accounts for more than one third of the state's residents. More than 1 in 10 California residents is of Asian descent, and African Americans make up about 7 percent of the population.

California's population **increased** by **more than 27 million** people from **1950 to 2010**.

Q What are some of the reasons that many people from other states and other countries are choosing to move to California?

The capitol building of California was completed in 1874.

State Government

California is governed under a state constitution that was adopted in 1879. Like the federal government, California's state government has three branches. The executive branch is headed by a governor, who is responsible for making sure that state laws are carried out. The governor is elected to a four-year term. Other elected officials of the executive branch include the lieutenant governor, secretary of state, treasurer, attorney general, and controller.

The legislature is composed of a state assembly of 80 members, and a state senate of 40 members. The judicial system is headed by the California Supreme Court, which consists of a chief justice and six associate justices. There are many lower courts in the state, which has the largest court system in the United States.

California is divided into 58 counties. Each county has its own elected board of supervisors. The counties usually have a sheriff, district attorney, and county clerk.

Richard Nixon was born in Yerba Buena, California. Before he became president, he served as a U.S. Senator for the state of California and as vice president.

California's state song is called
"I Love You, California."

*I love you, California,
you're the greatest state of all.
I love you in the winter,
summer, spring and in the fall.
I love your fertile valleys;
your dear mountains I adore.
I love your grand old ocean
and I love her rugged shore.
I love your redwood forests
love your fields of yellow grain,
I love your summer breezes,
and I love your winter rain,
I love you, land of flowers;
land of honey, fruit and wine,
I love you, California;
you have won this heart of mine.*

* excerpted

An electric reproduction of the capitol building's original gas chandelier from the late 1800s hangs in the California Senate Chamber.

Los Angeles has the largest Cinco de Mayo celebration in the world.

Celebrating Culture

More new immigrants settle in California than in any other state. Many different cultural groups live and work in California. Hispanic cultural influence, including foods from Mexico and Central America, can be found throughout the state. A large number of California cities have Spanish names, reflecting the importance of Spanish and Mexican influences.

San Francisco has one of the largest Chinese American populations of any city in the country. Each year in late January, or early February, Chinese New Year is celebrated with the Golden Dragon parade and fireworks. San Francisco's Chinese New Year originated in the 1860s, and today it is considered the largest Asian event in North America.

California is home to the largest African American population in the western United States, though fewer African Americans live in the West than in other regions of the country. Many African Americans moved to the state during World War II to find work. Their culture is felt strongly throughout the state, such as in the rise of hip-hop and R&B music culture.

The Chumash powwow in Malibu has been an annual cultural event for nearly 20 years.

The Chinese New Year parade in San Francisco has been named one of the world's top 10 parades by the International Festivals and Events Association.

Located on the Hollywood Walk of Fame, the TCL Chinese Theater originally opened in 1922.

Arts and Entertainment

California's involvement in the motion-picture industry, which is based in Hollywood, began in the early 1900s. In 1927, Walt Disney and his business partner, Ub Iwerks, created a mischievous mouse named Mickey. A short film with sound and music, *Steamboat Willie*, starred Mickey Mouse, with Disney himself providing the voice. Decades of popular films followed, and today the Walt Disney Company is one of the world's leading entertainment corporations.

California is a major center for the performing arts. It has many symphony orchestras, opera companies, and popular musicians. In the 1960s, the Beach Boys and other groups became famous for their music celebrating California's beaches and surfing culture. Today, many large music festivals take place in California, including the Coachella Valley Music and Arts Festival and the Outside Lands Music and Arts Festival.

Due to the booming entertainment, fashion, and hospitality industries, **Los Angeles** has the **16th biggest economy** in the **world**.

Founded in **1885**, Sacramento's **Crocker Art Museum** is the **oldest** operating **art museum** in the western United States.

The first film studio in Hollywood was opened on Sunset Boulevard in 1911. By 1915, Hollywood had become the center of the U.S. film industry. One **landmark** of the district is the famous TCL Chinese Theatre, which has footprints and handprints of celebrities in its **forecourt**. Many of the most famous celebrities in the world live in neighboring communities such as Bel Air and Beverly Hills.

Robert Redford is known as an iconic U.S. actor and director.

California has produced many writers, entertainers, and artists. San Francisco was the birthplace of the novelist Jack London, author of *The Call of the Wild*, and the poet Robert Frost, who won several Pulitzer Prizes. In the 1950s, the **Beat movement** began in San Francisco with poets and authors such as Jack Kerouac. Contemporary writer Amy Tan was born in Oakland. Academy Award-winning actor Robert Redford, born in Santa Monica, founded the Sundance Film Festival in 1978.

The Coachella festival is held annually in Indio, California. It is the largest music festival in the United States.

Sports and Recreation

California's warm climate and beautiful beaches help make swimming, sailing, and beach volleyball popular. Deep-sea diving allows people to view life in the ocean. California also has excellent locations for surfing and windsurfing. Due to California's climate, many outdoor recreational activities can be enjoyed year-round. Golf is particularly popular in the state. California has hundreds of golf courses, including the famous Pebble Beach course. With the dramatically different climates throughout the state, a person can go swimming in the ocean one day and then go skiing in nearby mountains the next.

Baseball legend **Joe DiMaggio** grew up in San Francisco and played minor league baseball in California before playing for the **New York Yankees**.

The first major **skateboarding** competition was held in Hermosa Beach in 1963.

That San Francisco 49ers were established in 1946. They play home games in Levi Stadium in Santa Clara, California.

California has far more professional sports teams than any other state. The state has three teams in the National Football League, five in Major League Baseball, four in the National Basketball Association, and three in the National Hockey League. There are also professional teams in soccer and women's basketball. The San Francisco 49ers football team was the first major league professional sports team in California. The Oakland Raiders and San Diego Chargers football teams have fans throughout the country. Basketball fans flock to see Los Angeles Lakers stars, such as Kobe Bryant, play at the Staples Center.

Pebble Beach Golf Course, outside of Carmel, has hosted golf tournaments since it opened in 1919.

San Francisco Bay offers some of the most challenging windsurfing conditions in the United States.

Get To Know CALIFORNIA

More **turkeys** are raised in California than in any other state.

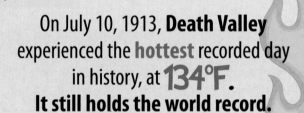

On July 10, 1913, **Death Valley** experienced the **hottest** recorded day in history, at 134°F. **It still holds the world record.**

The **Aquarium of the Pacific** in Long Beach is home to more than

12,000

ocean creatures.

California is the only state in the U.S. that has hosted both the **summer** and **winter** Olympics.

Fallbrook, CA, is the **Avocado Capital of the World** and celebrates with a yearly **avocado festival.**

Miners pulled more than *750,000* pounds of gold from California's ground during the **gold rush.**

MOUNT SHASTA AND LASSEN PEAK ARE BOTH ACTIVE VOLCANOES IN CALIFORNIA.

Brain Teasers

What have you learned about California after reading this book? Test your knowledge by answering these questions. All of the information can be found in the text you just read. The answers are provided below for easy reference.

1 What is California's state flower?

2 When was the California gold rush?

3 How tall can California redwood trees grow?

4 How fast can the California condor fly?

5 Which football team is located in Oakland, California?

6 Which treaty ended the Mexican-American War and gave California to the United States?

7 How many members does the state assembly have?

8 Where can famous handprints be found in Hollywood, California?

ANSWER KEY
1. The California Poppy 2. 1849 3. More than 350 feet tall 4. Up to 55 miles per hour 5. The Raiders 6. Treaty of Guadalupe Hidalgo 7. 80 8. TCL Chinese Theatre

Key Words

Beat movement: a social and literary movement in the 1950s

captivity: the state of being confined, rather than existing nature

conservation: protection of the environment

contiguous: sharing a common border

dialects: regional versions of a language

endangered: in danger of dying out

expedition: a long trip, usually to explore

forecourt: open area in front of a building

habitat: the place where a plant or animal lives

hydroelectricity: water-generated power

landmark: a place of historical or cultural importance

missionaries: people sent to another country to do charitable work and convert others to their religion

quarries: large areas from which stone is obtained

succulents: fleshy plants that are found in desert areas and that can store water in their leaves

Index

Log on to www.av2books.com

AV² by Weigl brings you media enhanced books that support active learning. Go to www.av2books.com, and enter the special code found on page 2 of this book. You will gain access to enriched and enhanced content that supplements and complements this book. Content includes video, audio, weblinks, quizzes, a slide show, and activities.

AV² Online Navigation

Book Pages
AV² pages directly correspond to pages in the book.

Audio
Listen to sections of the book read aloud.

Video
Watch informative video clips.

Embedded Weblinks
Gain additional information for research.

Key Words
Study vocabulary, and complete a matching word activity.

Try This!
Complete activities and hands-on experiments.

Quizzes
Test your knowledge.

Slide Show
View images and captions, and prepare a presentation.

AV² was built to bridge the gap between print and digital. We encourage you to tell us what you like and what you want to see in the future.

Sign up to be an AV² Ambassador at www.av2books.com/ambassador.